What is...

Inauguration Day

USA

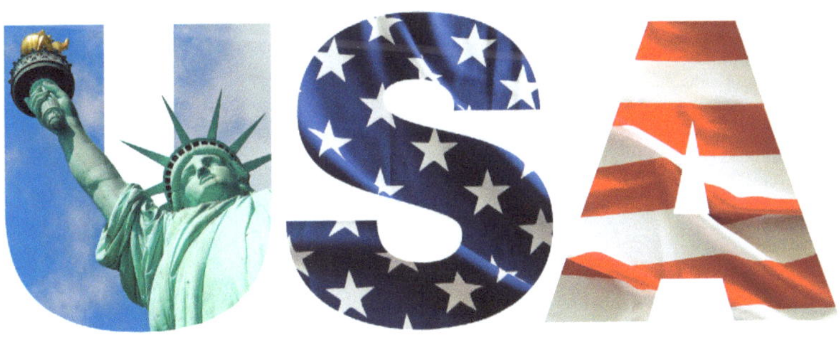

We the People
domestic Tranquility provide for the
Posterity, do ordain and establish
Article. I

Find Our Children's Books at Amazon, IngramSpark, Lulu, Barnes & Noble, Target, and Other Retailers Worldwide. Find Publishing & Consulting Services, Our Book Podcast, YouTube Channel, Educational Blog, and so much more at: www.SlothDreamsBooks.com or www.PictureBookPro.org

www.SlothDreamsBooks.com
www.PictureBookPro.org

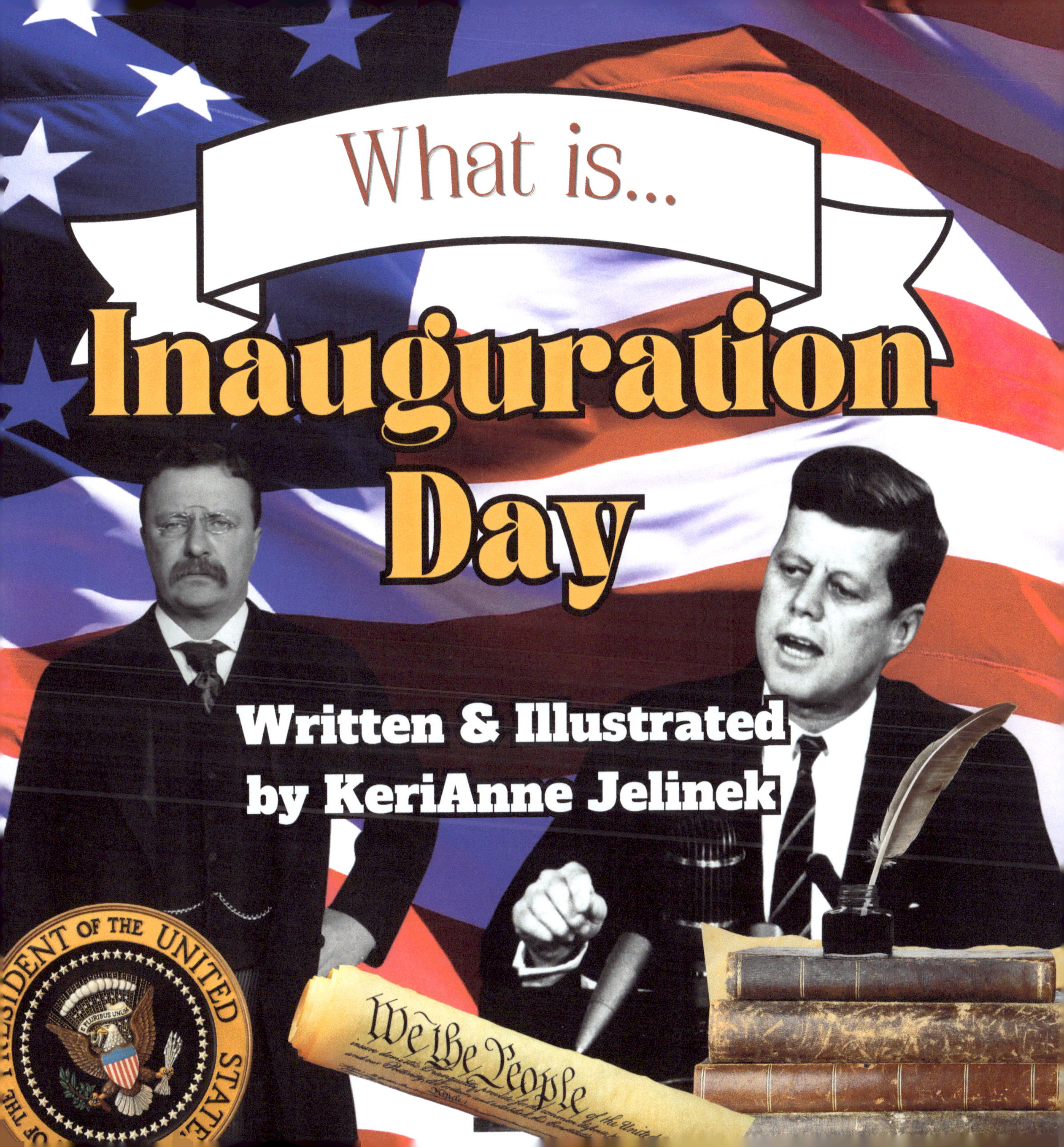

What is...
Inauguration Day
Written & Illustrated
by KeriAnne Jelinek
PRESIDENT OF THE UNITED STATES
E PLURIBUS UNUM
We The People

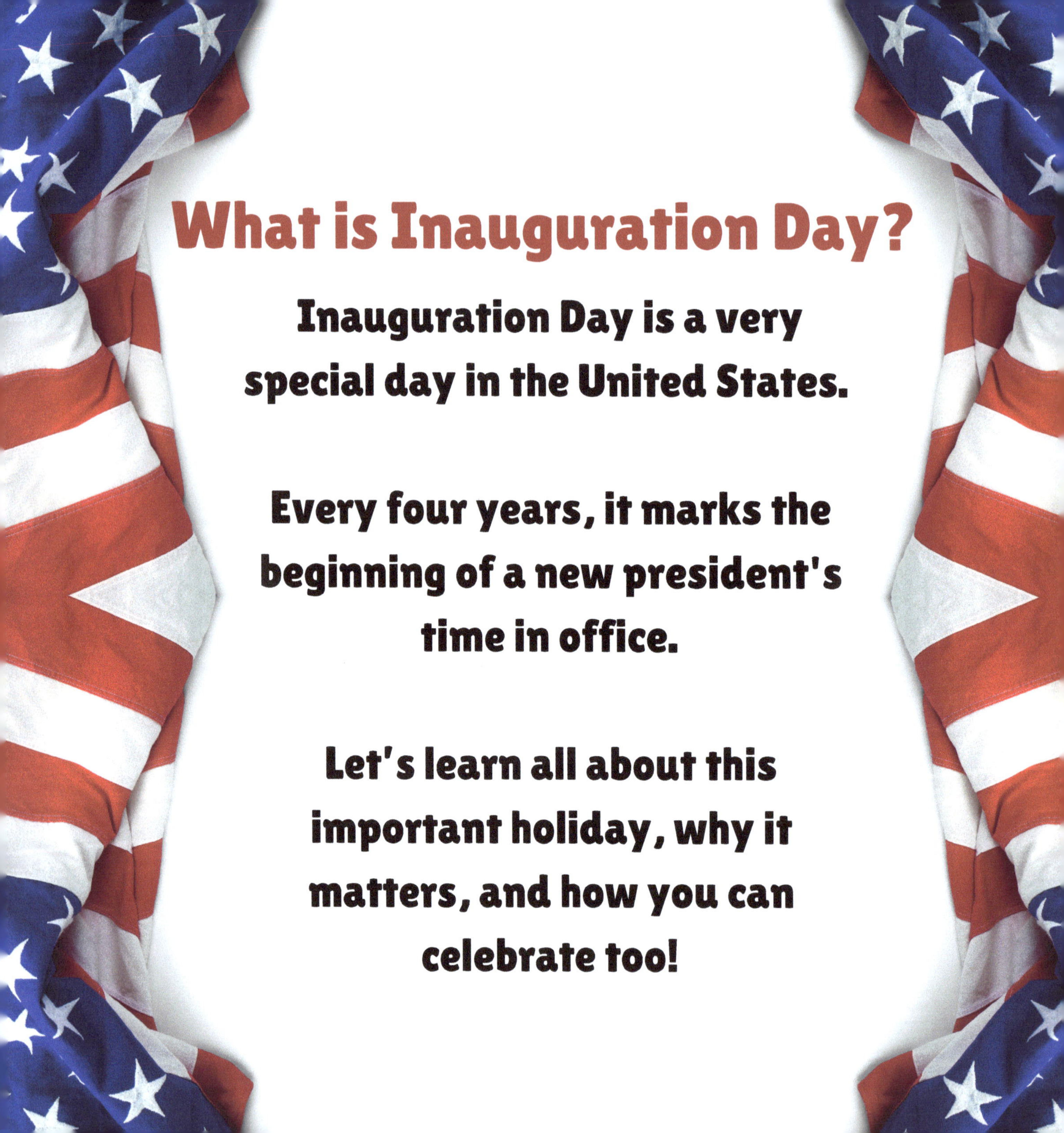

What is Inauguration Day?

Inauguration Day is a very special day in the United States.

Every four years, it marks the beginning of a new president's time in office.

Let's learn all about this important holiday, why it matters, and how you can celebrate too!

Inauguration Day happens every four years on or around January 20. On this day, the President of the United States officially starts their job as leader of the country. The Vice President begins their job, too!

Here are some fun facts and things that happen on Inauguration Day:

- **The Oath of Office** – **The president raises their right hand and promises to do their job well and protect the Constitution of the United States.**

- **The Capitol Building** – **The ceremony takes place in Washington, D.C., on the steps of the U.S. Capitol.**

- **Parades and Celebrations** – **After the oath, there's usually a big parade with bands, flags, and performances.**

- **A Peaceful Transition** – **One of the coolest things about Inauguration Day is how peaceful it is! It's a tradition that shows the world how democracy works in the U.S.**

- **First Inauguration** – **The very first Inauguration Day happened on April 30, 1789, when George Washington became the first president.**

- **A National Holiday for Unity** – **It's not just about the new president—it's a day for everyone to come together as a country.**

- **Special Speeches** – **The new president gives an "Inaugural Address," a speech where they share their hopes and plans for the future.**

- **Dressing Up** – **People wear their nicest clothes, and the president and vice president usually wear formal suits or dresses.**

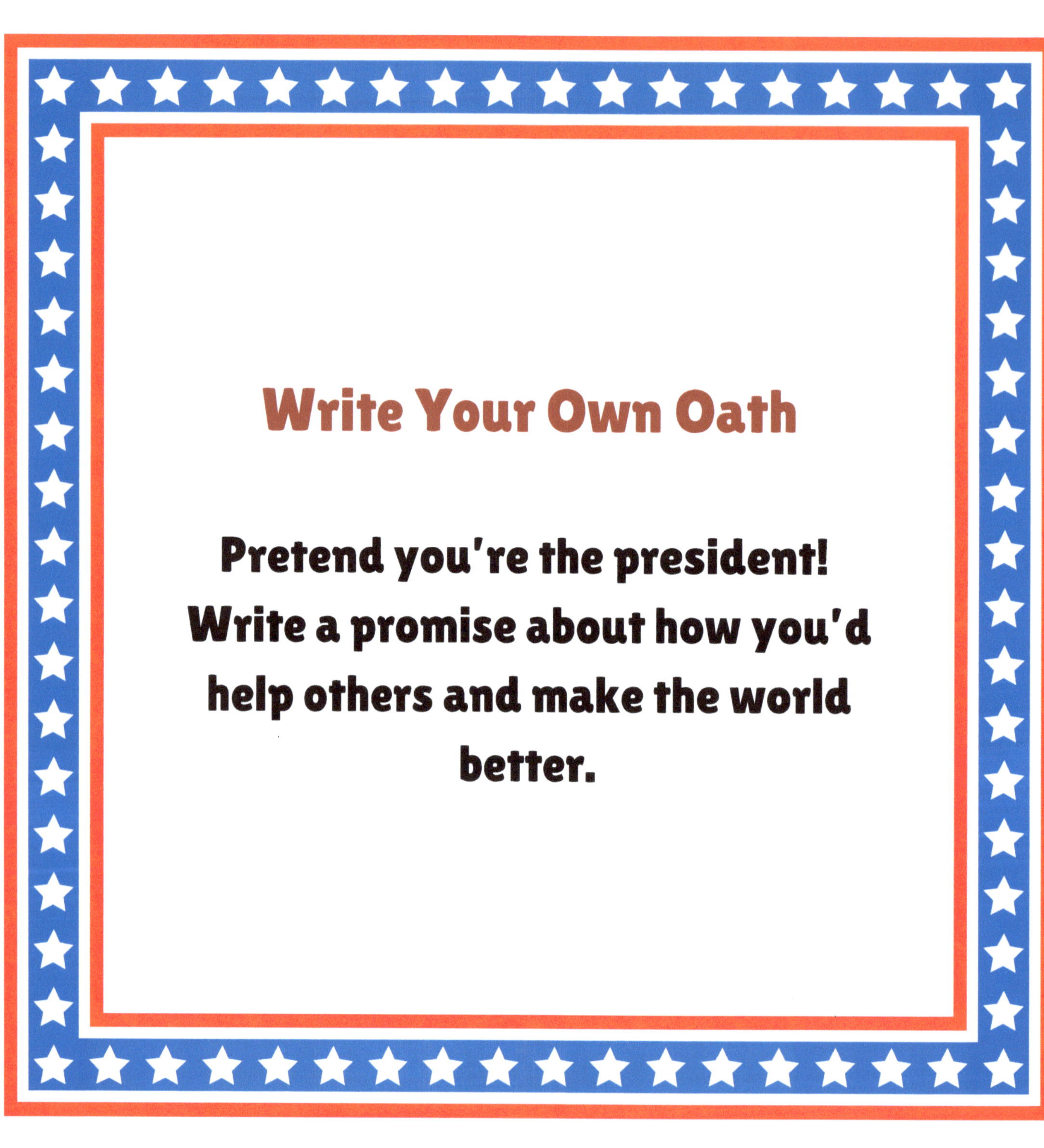

Write Your Own Oath

**Pretend you're the president!
Write a promise about how you'd
help others and make the world
better.**

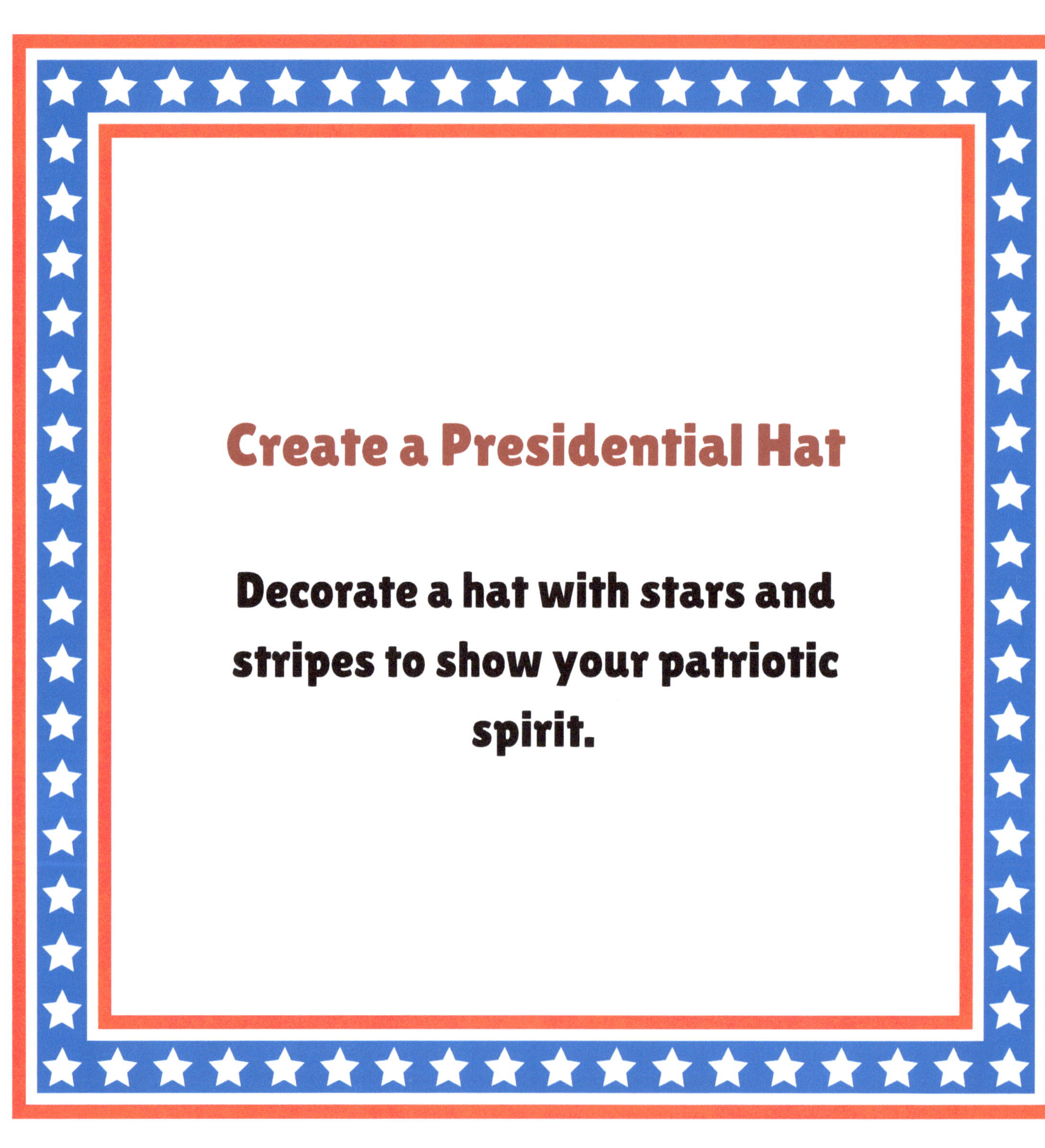

Create a Presidential Hat

Decorate a hat with stars and stripes to show your patriotic spirit.

Host a Parade

March around your house or yard with flags and music to celebrate.

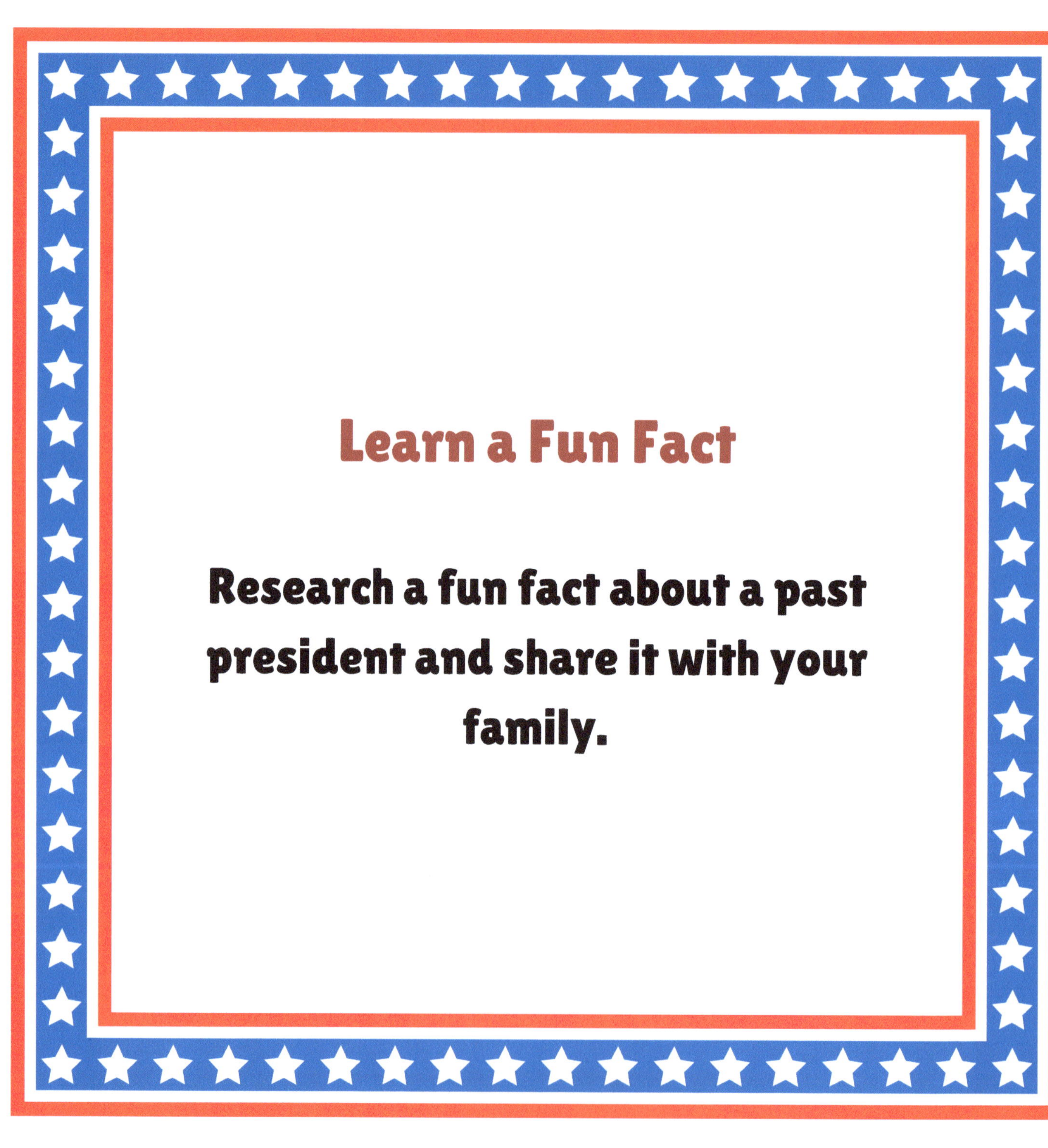

Learn a Fun Fact

Research a fun fact about a past president and share it with your family.

DID
YOU
KNOW
?

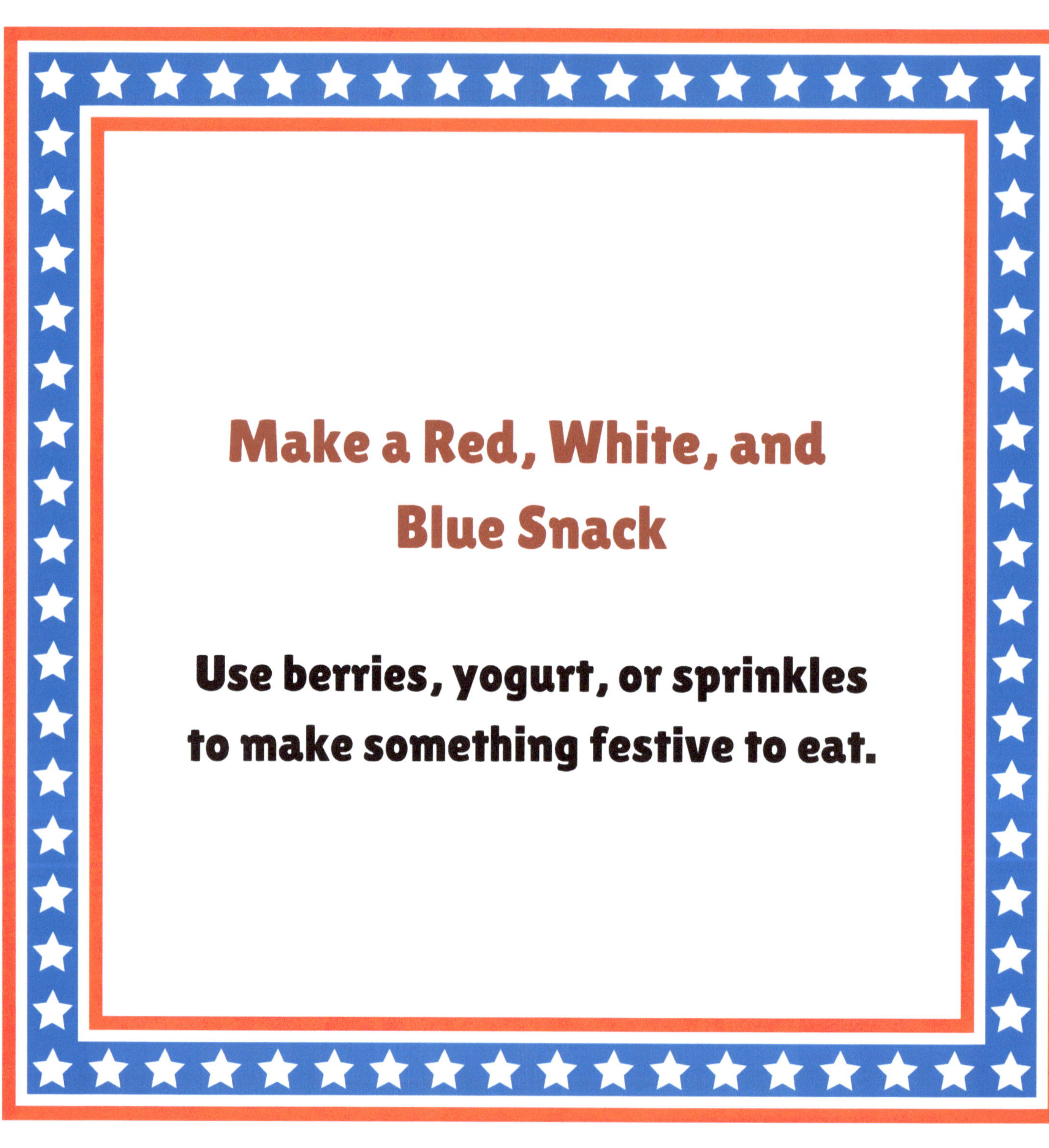

Make a Red, White, and Blue Snack

Use berries, yogurt, or sprinkles to make something festive to eat.

yum
yum

Draw the White House

Get creative and draw your own version of the president's home.

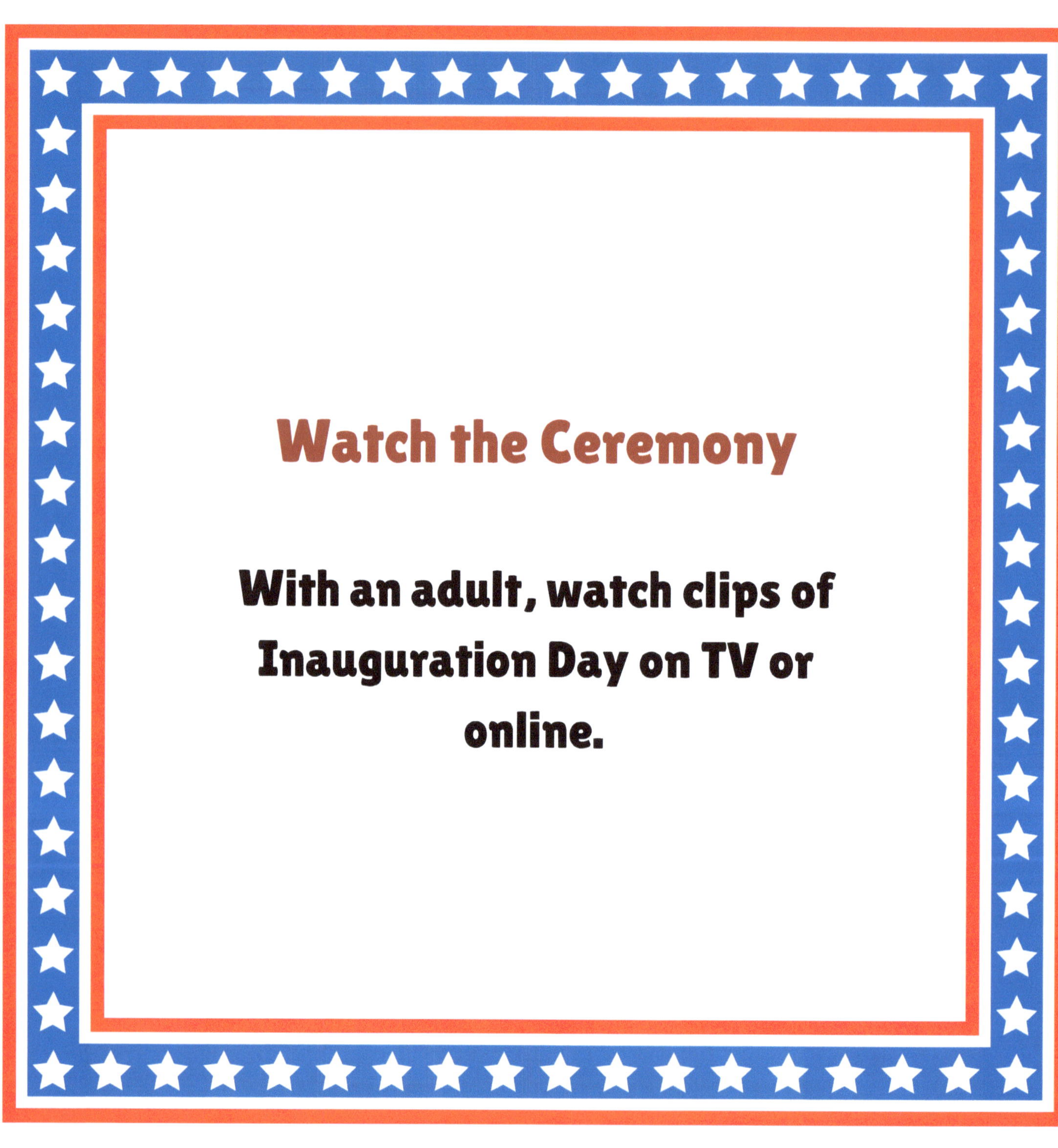

Watch the Ceremony

With an adult, watch clips of Inauguration Day on TV or online.

Plan a Speech

Write or say a short speech about something you care about, like protecting animals or helping the environment.

Craft a Flag

Make a paper flag to wave
during your celebration.

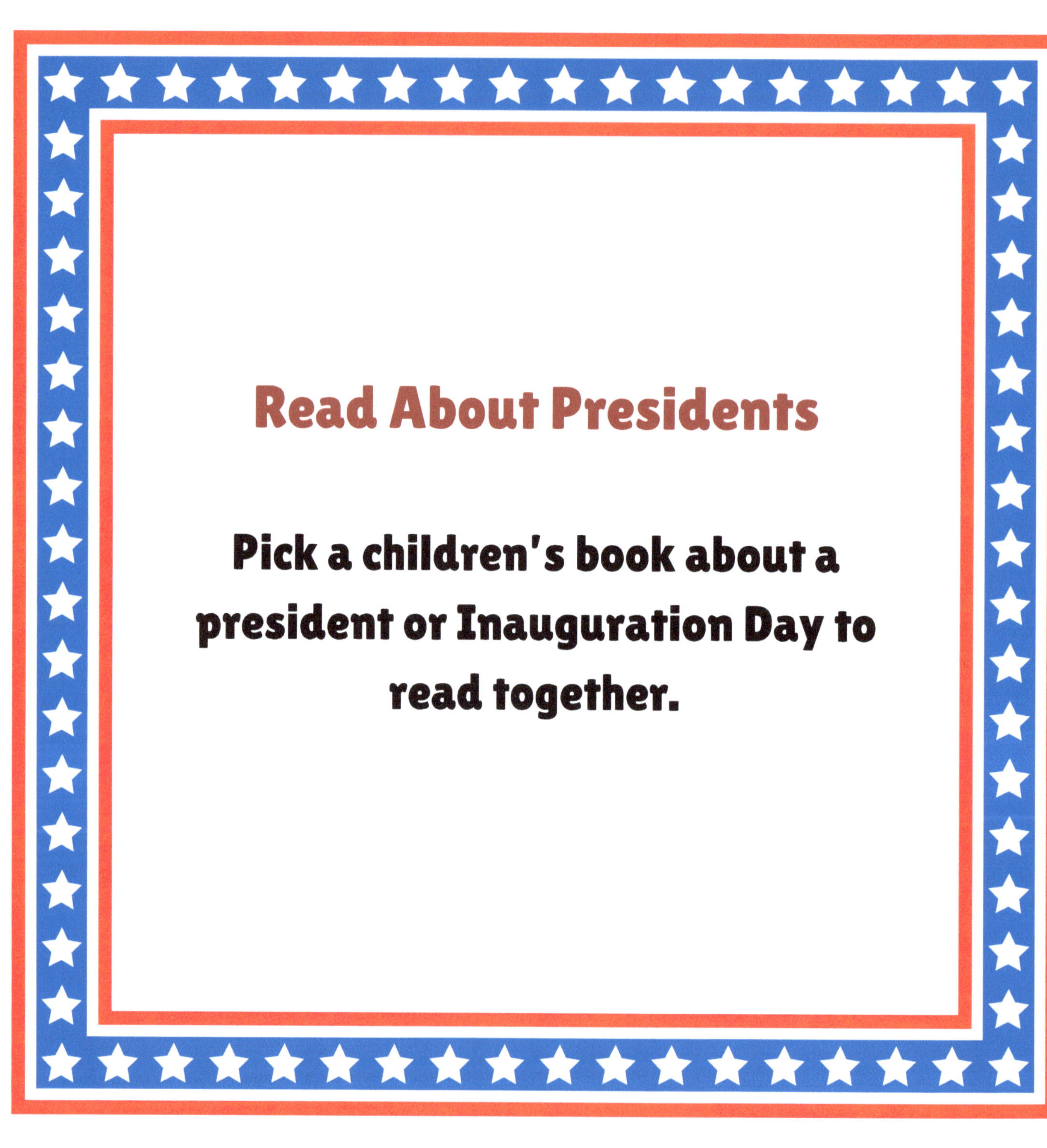

Read About Presidents

Pick a children's book about a president or Inauguration Day to read together.

PAST,
PRESENT
and FUTURE

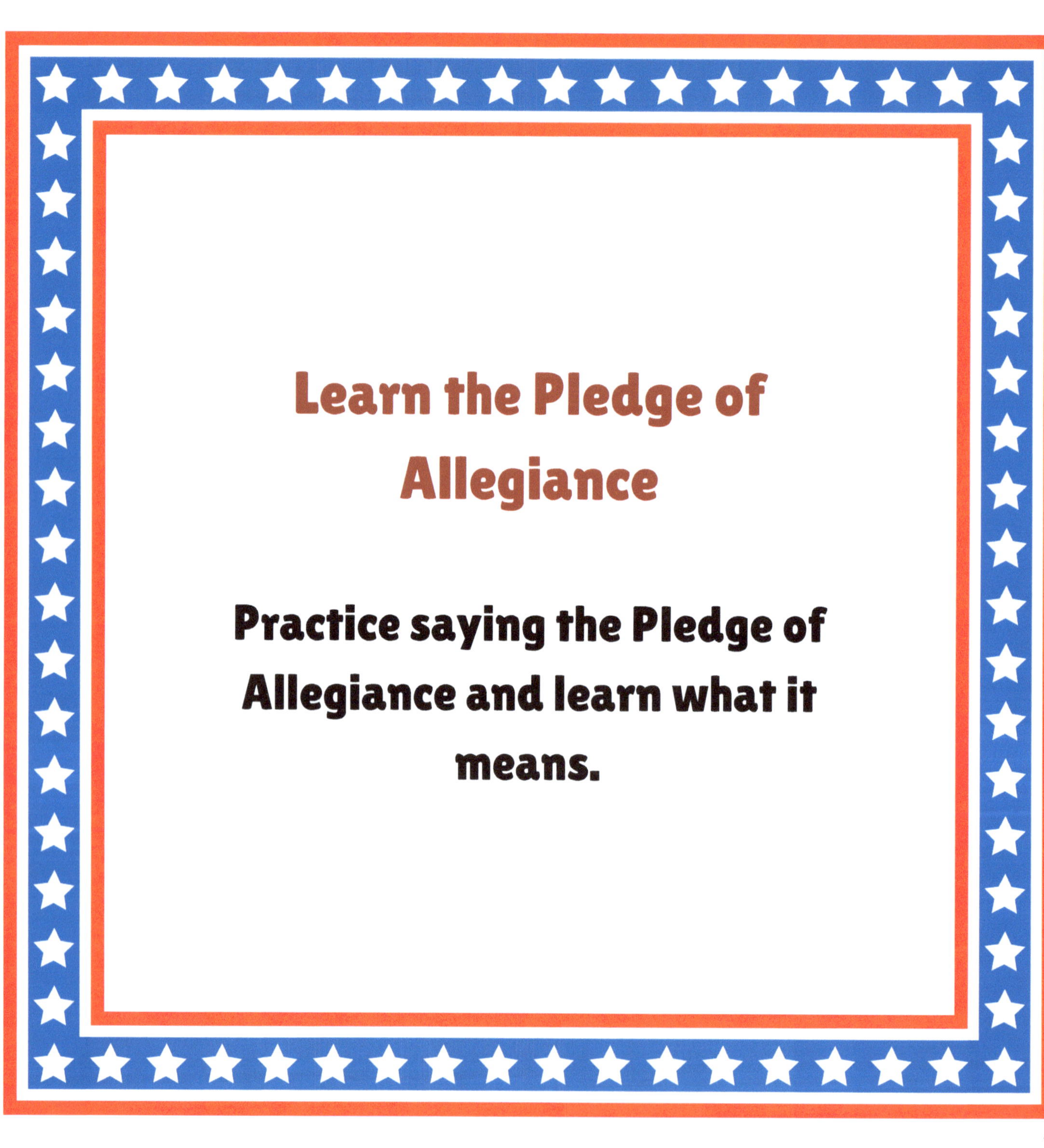

Learn the Pledge of Allegiance

Practice saying the Pledge of Allegiance and learn what it means.

Sing a Patriotic Song

Try singing "America the Beautiful" , "This Land Is Your Land", or the National Anthem.

Decorate Your Space

Use red, white, and blue
streamers to decorate a room.

Freedom

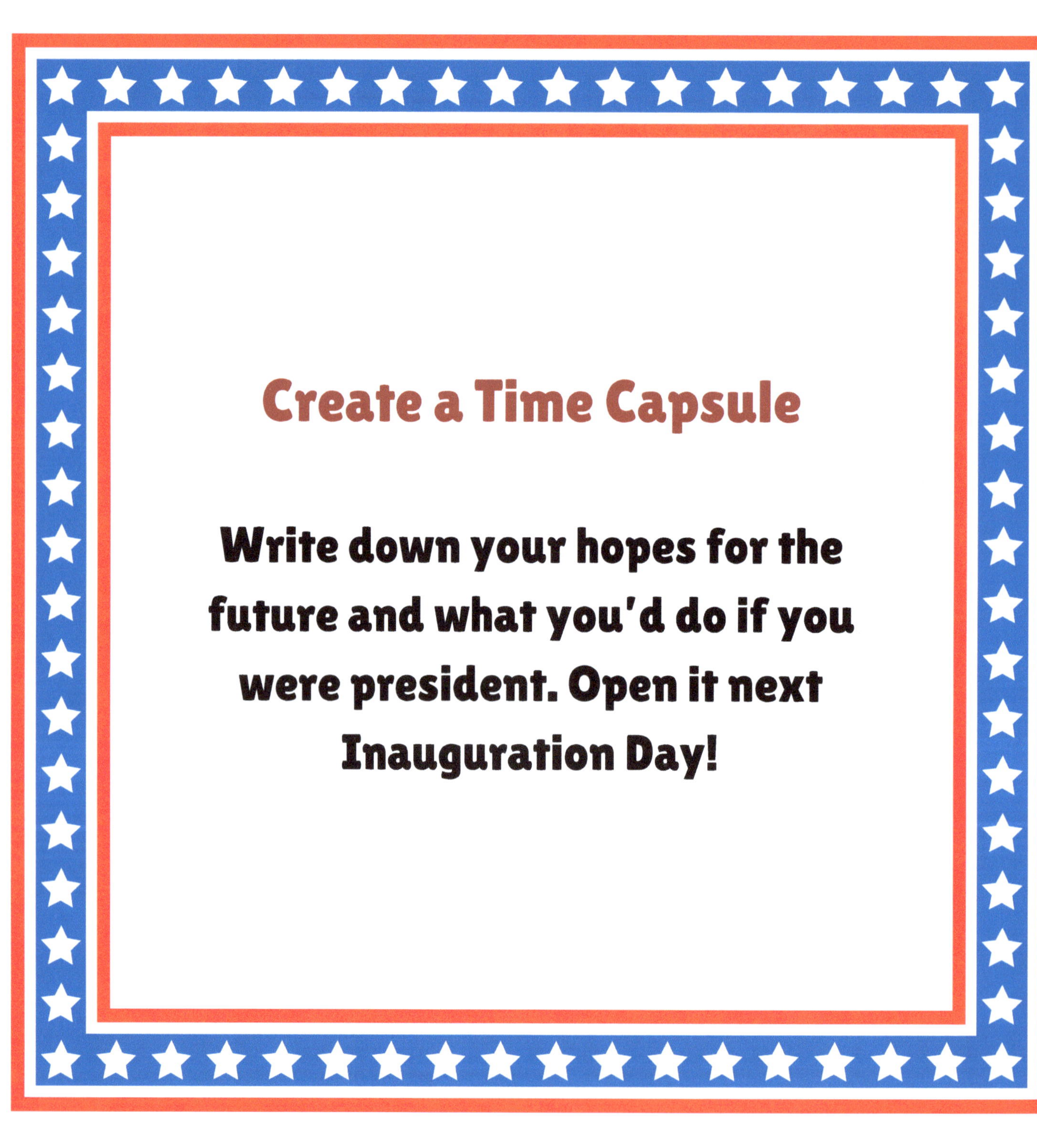
Create a Time Capsule

Write down your hopes for the future and what you'd do if you were president. Open it next Inauguration Day!

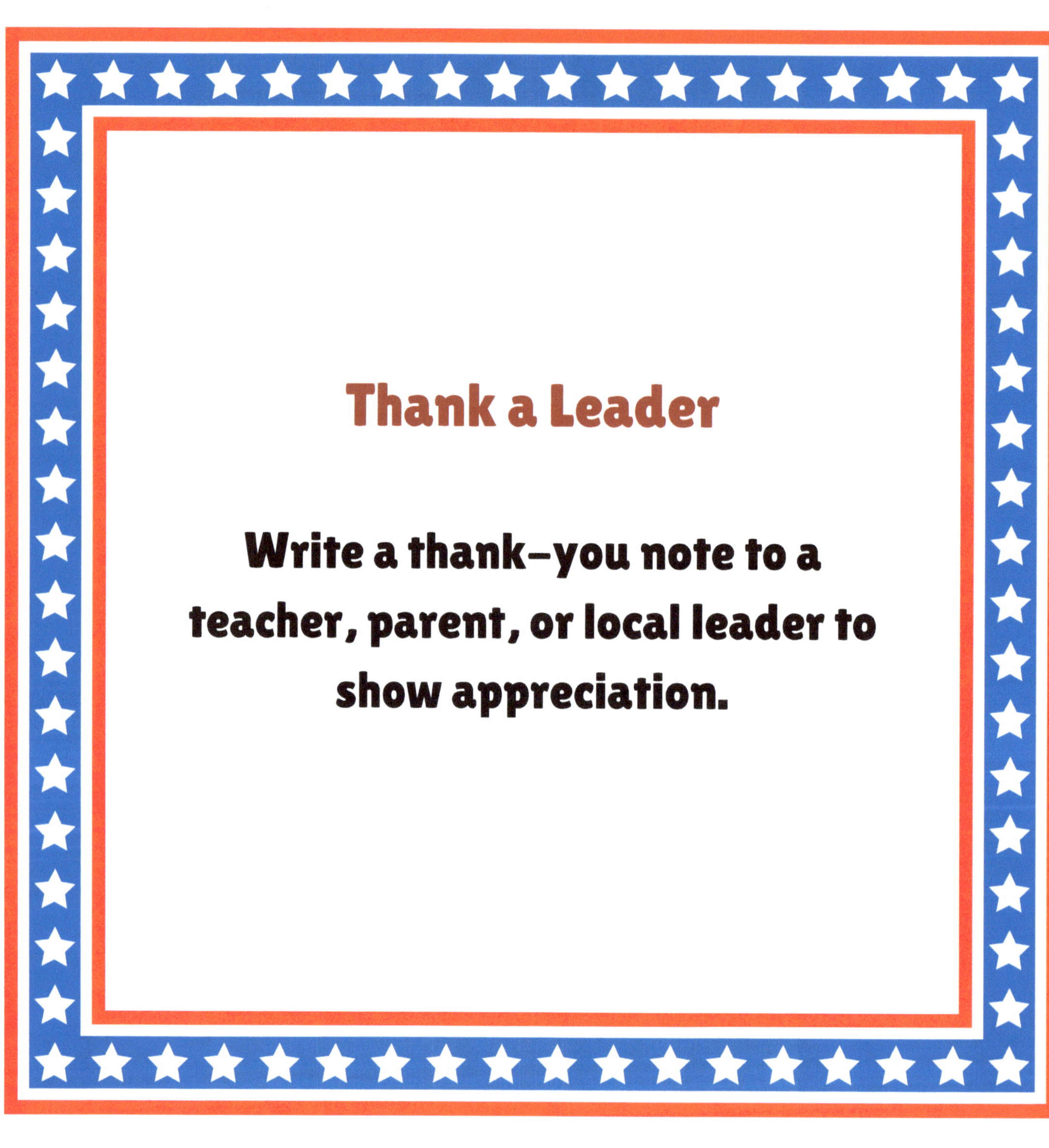

Thank a Leader

Write a thank–you note to a teacher, parent, or local leader to show appreciation.

Thank
You
THANK YOU
STAR